eyewonder
Stars and Planets

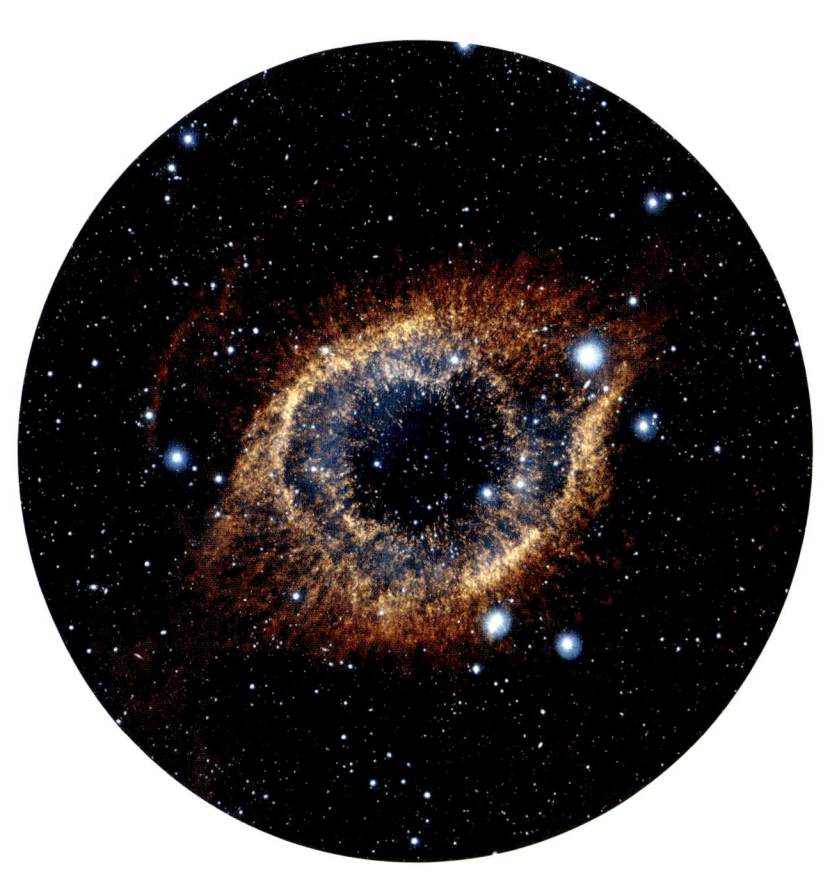

THIRD EDITION
Senior Art Editor Ragini Rawat
Project Editor Upamanyu Das
Editor Zarak Rais
Art Editor Diya Varma
Picture Researcher Ridhima Sikka
Deputy Manager, Picture Research Virien Chopra
Managing Editor Kingshuk Ghoshal
Managing Art Editors Govind Mittal, Anna Hall
Pre-production Designer Dheeraj Singh
Pre-production Image Editor Mohd Rizwan
Production Editor Vishal Bhatia
Production Controller Jack Matts
Senior Jackets Art Editor Nehal Verma
Project Jackets Art Editor Vidushi Chaudhry
DK Delhi Creative Head Malavika Talukder
Associate Publisher Gemma Farr
Art Director Mabel Chan

Consultant Giles Sparrow

FIRST EDITION
Written and edited by Simon Holland
Designed by Tanya Tween, Claire Penny, Tory Gordon-Harris
Publishing Manager Mary Ling
Managing Art Editor Rachael Foster
Consultant Carole Stott

This edition published in 2025
First published in Great Britain in 2001 by
Dorling Kindersley Limited
20 Vauxhall Bridge Road,
London, SW1V 2SA

The authorised representative in the EEA is
Dorling Kindersley Verlag GmbH. Arnulfstr. 124,
80636 Munich, Germany

Copyright © 2001, 2015, 2025 Dorling Kindersley Limited
A Penguin Random House Company
10 9 8 7 6 5 4 3 2 1
001–348663–Oct/2025

All rights reserved.
No part of this publication may be reproduced, stored in or introduced into a retrieval system, or transmitted, in any form, or by any means (electronic, mechanical, photocopying, recording, or otherwise), without the prior written permission of the copyright owner.

No part of this publication may be used or reproduced in any manner for the purpose of training artificial intelligence technologies or systems. In accordance with Article 4(3) of the DSM Directive 2019/790, DK expressly reserves this work from the text and data mining exception.

A CIP catalogue record for this book
is available from the British Library.
ISBN: 978-0-2417-3232-8

Printed and bound in China

www.dk.com

Contents

4–5
Our place in space

6–7
A closer look

8–9
The Moon

10–11
The Sun

12–13
Solar System

14–15
Hothouse planets

16–17
The red planet

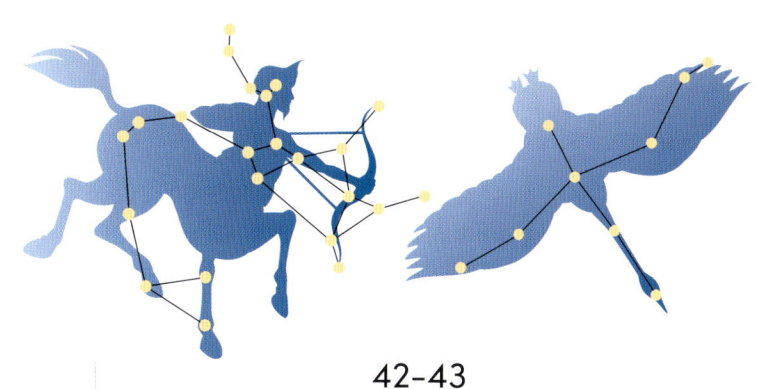

18-19
Rocky racetrack

20-21
Jupiter

22-23
Ringed wonder

24-25
Ice giants

26-27
Many moons

28-29
Edge of the Solar System

30-31
Exoplanets

32-33
Life of stars

34-35
Types of stars

36-37
Constellations

38-39
Families of stars

40-41
All about the Universe

42-43
Exploring space

44-45
Life in orbit

46-47
Our future in space

48-49
Stargazers

50-51
What's this?

52-53
Space race

54-55
Glossary

56
Index and Acknowledgments

Our place in space

We are among millions of living things on the rocky planet known as Earth. Our world loops around a star we call the Sun, in a fixed path called an orbit. There are countless stars in the vast expanse of space called the Universe.

Earth is surrounded by a protective blanket of air called the atmosphere.

Home planet
Earth is one of eight planets that orbit the Sun, held in place by a strong invisible force called gravity. Most of our world is covered in water. It is also at just the right distance from the Sun, neither too close nor too far. This helps life exist on Earth.

Sun and Moon
During the day, our planet is lit up by the Sun. At night, the brightest thing in the sky is the Moon, which reflects the Sun's light. The Moon is a rocky object that orbits our planet.

Sunlight   Moonlight

Look up!

What do you see when you look up on a clear night? Most of the lights you can see in the night sky are stars like the Sun. They appear faint because they are so far away. See them more clearly with a tool called a telescope!

 ## WHAT IS A STAR?

A star is a giant ball of superhot gas. In its core, it uses up hydrogen gas to make helium gas, giving off lots of energy in the form of light and heat. Scientists measure the great distances to the stars in light years. A light year is the distance travelled by a star's light in a year.

What is space?

Space is everything in the Universe outside Earth's atmosphere. This includes objects such as other stars and planets, but also clouds of gas, and huge areas without anything.

All the light in space comes from stars.

A closer look

There's magic in the twinkling night sky. For thousands of years, humans wondered about these lights, which we now know as stars. Four hundred years ago, space scientists called astronomers made the first telescopes to help them peer deeper into space, revealing that we are part of a much larger Universe.

The constellation of Orion, the Hunter

Starry pictures
Early astronomers imagined pictures made by linking stars in the sky. They called them constellations. Today, we know of 88 constellations.

Using telescopes
A telescope is an instrument that collects light coming from distant space objects using lenses or mirrors. It can make objects look bigger, brighter, or clearer than our eyes can see, revealing details hidden to our eyes.

 INVISIBLE WONDERS

The light our eyes see (visible light) is just one kind of "radiation" energy. Objects in space also produce other types of radiation – such as infrared – which may have less or more energy than light, and are invisible to the human eye. These types of radiation can only be viewed by special cameras and telescopes.

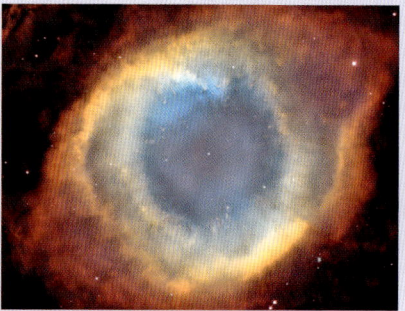

Visible light image

Infrared image

The FAST dish is as big as 30 football fields!

Radio telescopes

The biggest telescopes of all detect radio waves (invisible radiation with much less energy than light). Astronomers collect radio waves using huge dishes, such as this one at China's FAST radio telescope.

James Webb Space Telescope

Eyes in the sky

Earth's atmosphere soaks up light, blurring our view of space. Astronomers get around this problem by using large telescopes located on high mountains, where the air is thinner and clearer. Telescopes in space give us the sharpest and most detailed pictures of the Universe.

Mauna Kea Observatory located on top of the Mauna Kea volcano in Hawai'i

The Moon

On most clear nights, you can find a constant companion in our sky – our Moon! This rocky world is Earth's only natural satellite (an object that orbits another in space). Many spacecraft have visited it, including the crewed Apollo missions that took 12 astronauts to the Moon.

Explosive beginning

Astronomers think the Moon formed from rock flung out by a collision between Earth and a smaller planet about 4.5 billion years ago.

Silvery face

The Moon takes just over 27 days to go around Earth, and spins exactly once in the same time. The same half of the Moon, called the "near side", always faces towards Earth.

US astronaut Alan Shepard marks the Apollo 14 landing site on the Moon in 1971.

Near side

Smooth, dark areas of the surface are called "seas" – but they are entirely dry.

Von Neumann is a large impact crater on the Moon's far side.

👁 CHANGING SHAPE

New Moon | Cresent | First Quarter | Gibbous | Full Moon

Why does the Moon appear to change its shape over a month? As the Moon orbits our planet, the Sun lights up different amounts of its near side. Over a period of 29 days, it grows from a thin banana to a dinner plate, and back again. On a "new Moon", we can't see the Moon at all!

Hidden side

The far side of the Moon faces away from Earth. Humans only saw it for the first time in 1959, when the Luna 3 space probe sent pictures back to Earth.

Impacts from space rock over billions of years have left the Moon riddled with craters.

Lunar explorer

Many robotic spacecraft have studied the Moon. In 2019, China's Yutu-2 rover became the first robot on the lunar surface to explore the Moon's far side.

Far side

The Sun

Our Sun is a star: a huge ball of gas burning at temperatures so hot they are hard to imagine. It is the nearest star to Earth, and its heat and light are what make life on Earth possible.

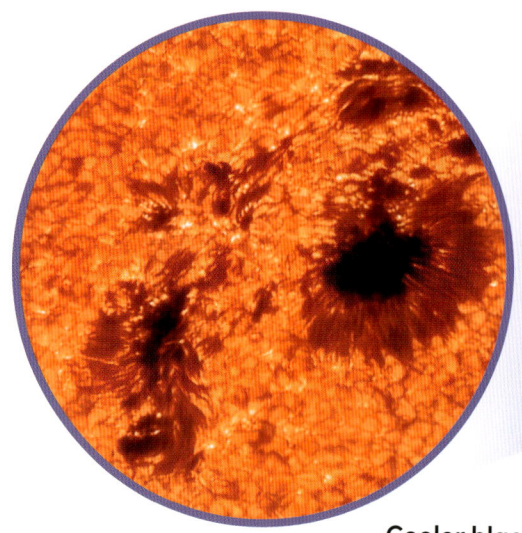

Cooler black patches on the Sun's surface are called sunspots.

Studying the Sun

The Parker Solar Probe is a robotic spacecraft that flies close to the Sun, to learn more about it. Its heavy shield protects it from the star's incredible heat.

Solar eclipse

The Moon spins around Earth. It can sometimes come between the Sun and our planet, blocking the star's light. This causes a solar eclipse.

👁 THE SEASONS

Earth is tilted, not straight. As it moves in circles around the Sun, different parts of our planet receive different amounts of sunlight. This creates seasons: summer is when a part of the world gets the most light, and winter is when it gets least.

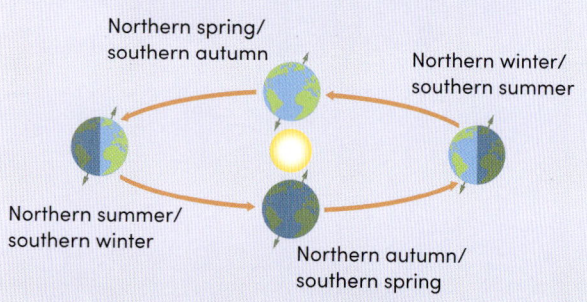

Northern spring/ southern autumn

Northern winter/ southern summer

Northern summer/ southern winter

Northern autumn/ southern spring

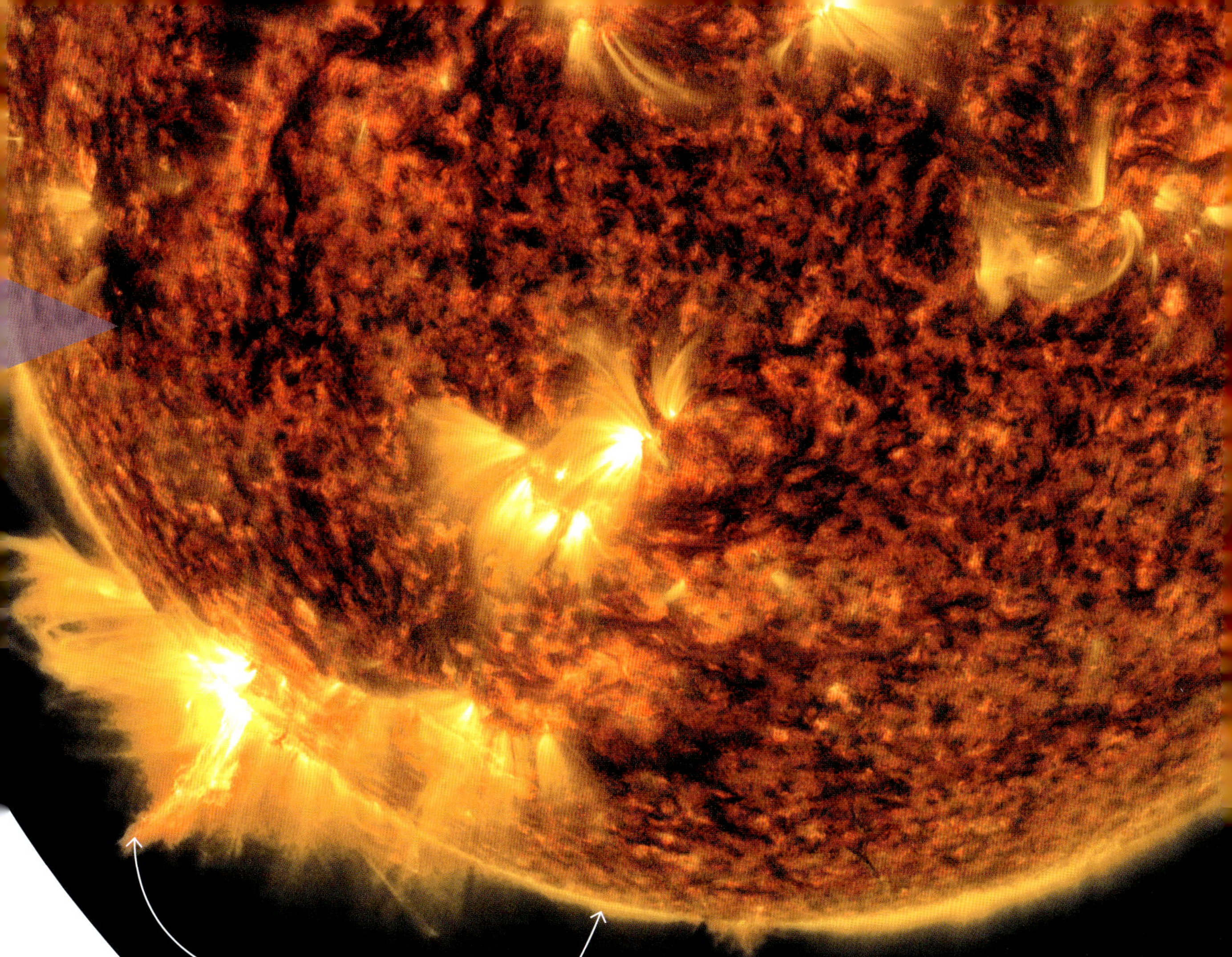

Streams of thick gas are flung out into space.

The Sun has a thin, hot atmosphere called the corona.

Ball of energy
The Sun is a giant ball of burning hydrogen gas, with a fiery furnace at its centre. Energy moves up and out from the centre, creating a constantly changing surface. The light we see is the Sun's energy escaping into space.

Glowing skies
When particles from the Sun hit Earth's atmosphere, it can create shifting patterns of light called auroras. These beautiful light displays usually happen in Earth's polar regions.

Solar System

Our Sun is far from alone in space. It is surrounded by a large family of objects, some rocky or icy, others made of gas! Eight large worlds called planets loop around it in orbits. Many of them have smaller companions called moons. Other objects in our Solar System include dwarf planets, asteroids, and comets.

Kuiper Belt

The Sun's family

A planet is an object with enough material to become a sphere that orbits a star. The four planets closest to the Sun are small and rocky, while the ones further out are much bigger and made up of gas and ice. Space rocks called asteroids are mainly found between Mars and Jupiter. Further out beyond Neptune is a belt of icy comets and other objects.

👁 IN THE BEGINNING

The Solar System formed when a huge cloud of gas and dust collapsed and formed the Sun, about 4.5 billion years ago. The material left behind from this cloud formed a flat spinning disc, which gave rise to the planets and other objects in the Solar System.

The closer a planet is to the Sun, the faster it moves along its orbit.

The planets line up along a path called the ecliptic.

Mars • Uranus • Jupiter • Earth's Moon • Neptune • Saturn • Venus

Planetary parade

As we look up from Earth, we may see the planets as bright dots in different places in the night sky. But on some special nights, they line up, forming a glorious planetary parade.

A year on Earth is as long as four years on Mercury!

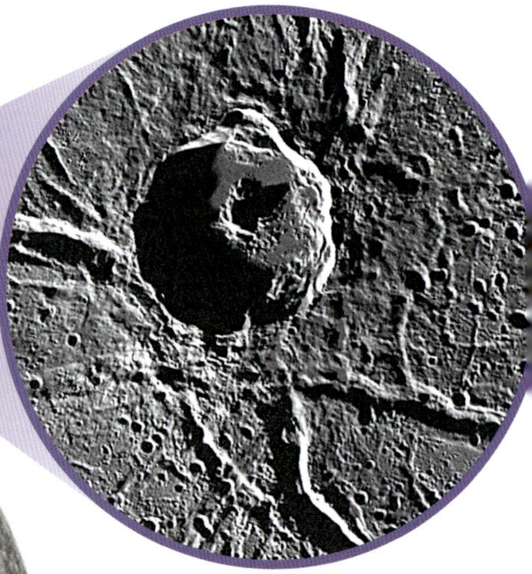

The Apollodorus Crater is surrounded by deep cracks, which make it look like a spider.

Fry or freeze
Mercury is the closest planet to the Sun and the smallest one in the Solar System. It has no layer of air around it, which makes it boiling hot in the daytime and freezing cold at night.

Speedy target
Mercury moves through space much faster than Earth does. To reach it, robotic spacecraft such as BepiColombo must first swing past Venus to pick up speed.

👁 HOW HOT DOES IT GET?

Venus is a very hot planet, while Mercury is both hotter and colder than Earth, with the widest range of temperatures in our Solar System.

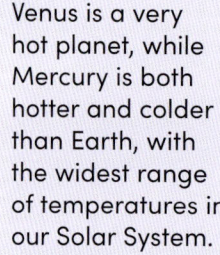
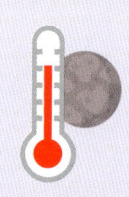

Mercury 430°C (806°F) Venus 464°C (867°F) Earth 57°C (134°F)

Hothouse planets

Mercury and Venus are the two planets closest to the searing heat of the Sun. They are both made of a mixture of rock and metals, and have a hard outer layer called a crust.

Stormy winds keep Venus' clouds moving.

Venus has a number of volcanoes. The biggest is called Maat Mons.

A scorched world

Venus is the second planet away from the Sun. It has a thick layer of gases around it that trap heat, making it extremely hot. A layer of bright clouds in Venus' atmosphere makes the surface hard to see.

Venus is nearly the same size as Earth.

Bright planet

Did you know that Venus is the second-brightest object in the night sky after the Moon? It can be seen looping through the morning sky before sunrise, and through the evening sky after sunset.

The red planet

On clear nights, Mars is a bright red dot in our sky. The rusty red dust on its surface and in its atmosphere makes it look like a hot desert world – but it is colder than Earth.

Taking off
A robot helicopter called Ingenuity was carried to Mars by a rover called Perseverance. Between 2021 and 2024, this robot made 72 short flights on Mars. It was the first vehicle to fly on another planet.

👁 BIG BREAKUP
Mars has two small moons – Phobos and Deimos. Phobos orbits very close to the planet, and gets slightly closer with each orbit. In 30-50 million years, Martian gravity will tear it apart, spreading its rocky chunks into a ring around the planet.

Phobos in orbit today

The moon breaks up

A ring forms

Powerful cameras help the rover capture photos.

Exploring Mars
Many space probes have visited Mars, including several wheeled robots called rovers. The rover Perseverance landed in 2021 to study rocks and look for signs of life on Mars.

Changing world

Mars is a mix of crater-covered hills and smooth sandy deserts. Billions of years ago, it had a thicker, warmer atmosphere and water on its surface.

Olympus Mons is a huge dormant volcano, three times taller than Mount Everest – Earth's tallest mountain.

Valles Marineris is a canyon system four times deeper than the Grand Canyon in the USA.

Blue skies

The red dust in the Martian atmosphere causes a dusty pink daytime sky. As the Sun goes down, the sky changes colour to a bluish glow, giving Mars a blue sunset!

Shooting stars
When space rocks plunge into Earth's atmosphere, they burn up. This creates streaks of light known as meteors, or shooting stars. If any chunks of rock reach Earth's surface, they are called meteorites.

Made of metal and heavier than a whale, the Hoba meteorite in northern Namibia is the largest ever found on Earth.

Rocky racetrack

Did you know our Solar System contains millions of rocky objects much smaller than planets or their moons? They are called asteroids. Many of them race around the Sun in a band called the Asteroid Belt.

Roaming rocks
Asteroids are bits of rock left over from when the Sun and planets formed. Most of them move in the Asteroid Belt – a band of space between the orbits of Mars and Jupiter.

 CERES

The largest object in the Asteroid Belt is Ceres. It is so big that it is known as a dwarf planet. Ceres was studied by the Dawn space probe between 2015 and 2018.

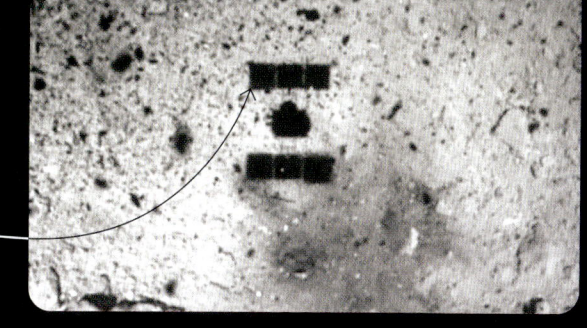

Shadow of Hayabusa2 on Ryugu

Asteroid explorer

Scientists study asteroids to learn more about how the rocky planets were formed. The Hayabusa2 space probe took pictures of the asteroid Ryugu's surface and brought back rock samples to Earth for study.

Sun

Asteroids can crash into each other as they orbit the Sun.

Earth

The Great Red Spot is a giant, whirling storm 1.3 times larger than Earth.

Jupiter, as seen by the Juno space probe

Jupiter

The largest planet in the Solar System, Jupiter is so big that all the other planets could fit inside it with room to spare. Wrapped in bands of colourful, fast-moving clouds, this gas giant makes one full spin in less than 10 hours.

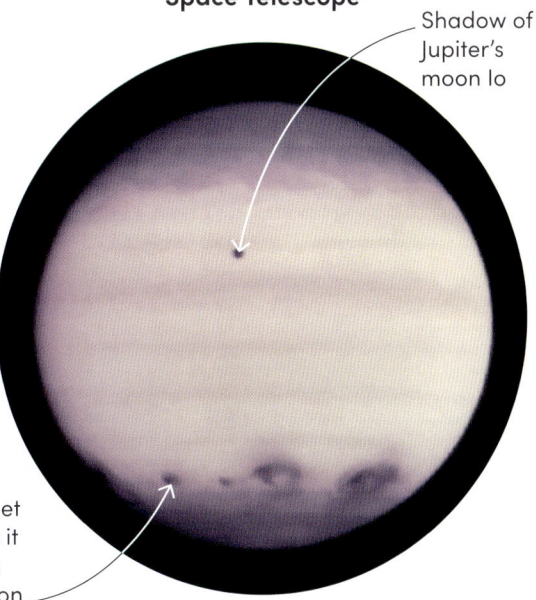

Ultraviolet light image of Jupiter taken by Hubble Space Telescope

Shadow of Jupiter's moon Io

Marks left by the comet Shoemaker-Levy 9 as it punched into Jupiter's atmosphere on collision

Ball of gas
Jupiter is a type of planet called a "gas giant", which is different from a rocky planet such as Earth. Gas giants are made up of lightweight gas held together by gravity.

Great protector
Jupiter's immense gravity protects Earth by drawing in many objects such as comets. Instead of smashing into Earth or the other inner planets, they crash harmlessly into Jupiter's clouds.

Mission to Jupiter
Juno is the latest space probe to study Jupiter. It makes short, high-speed flights above the clouds to see the giant planet closer than ever before.

Dazzling display
Fast-moving particles blowing out from the Sun are captured by Jupiter's powerful pull. They enter the planet's atmosphere near its poles, creating glowing auroras.

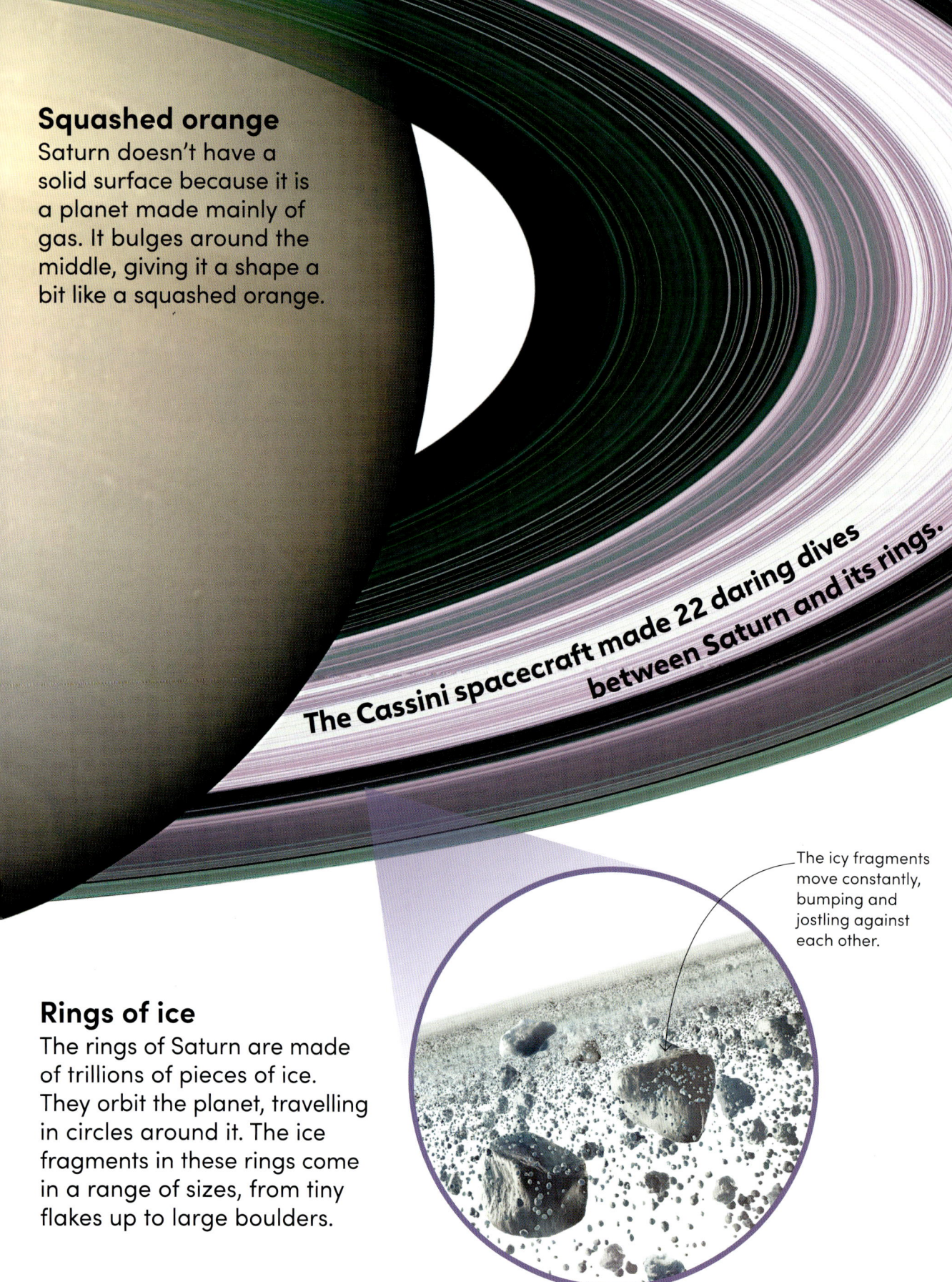

Squashed orange
Saturn doesn't have a solid surface because it is a planet made mainly of gas. It bulges around the middle, giving it a shape a bit like a squashed orange.

The Cassini spacecraft made 22 daring dives between Saturn and its rings.

The icy fragments move constantly, bumping and jostling against each other.

Rings of ice
The rings of Saturn are made of trillions of pieces of ice. They orbit the planet, travelling in circles around it. The ice fragments in these rings come in a range of sizes, from tiny flakes up to large boulders.

Ringed wonder

Giant rings of ice and dust loop around Saturn, the second-largest planet in the Solar System. It is the most distant world you can see with your eyes from Earth. This gas giant is surrounded by a huge family of moons.

Saturn's rings stretch across a distance more than twice as wide as Saturn itself.

Final descent
The Cassini spacecraft spent 13 years studying the ringed planet. When its mission ended in 2017, it plunged into Saturn, destroying itself. This was to make sure it didn't hit and damage any of Saturn's moons.

Many moons
Saturn has the most moons in the Solar System. Some are larger than Mercury, while others are much smaller. This photograph taken by Cassini shows just five of them.

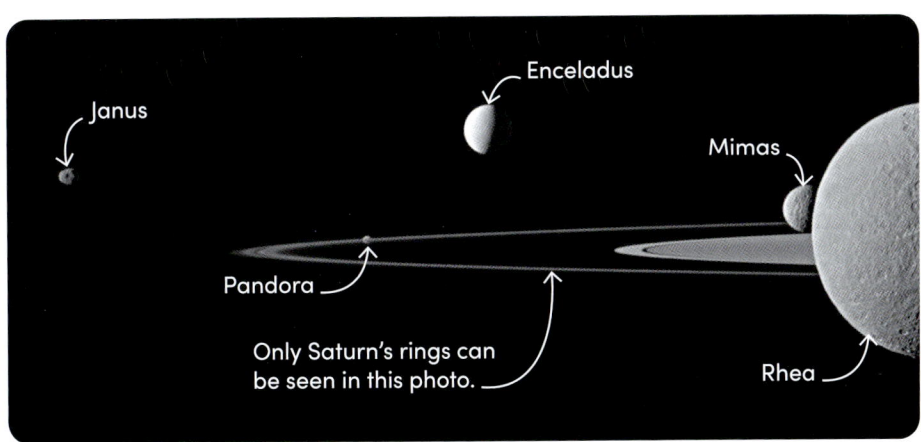

Janus

Enceladus

Mimas

Pandora

Only Saturn's rings can be seen in this photo.

Rhea

Ice giants

Sunlight takes almost three hours to reach the distant world of Uranus and four hours to reach colder Neptune. These giant planets are made mostly of slushy ice, so astronomers call them "ice giants".

Tilted planet

Uranus was the first planet discovered with a telescope. It goes around the Sun while tipped on one side, perhaps due to a huge collision early in its history.

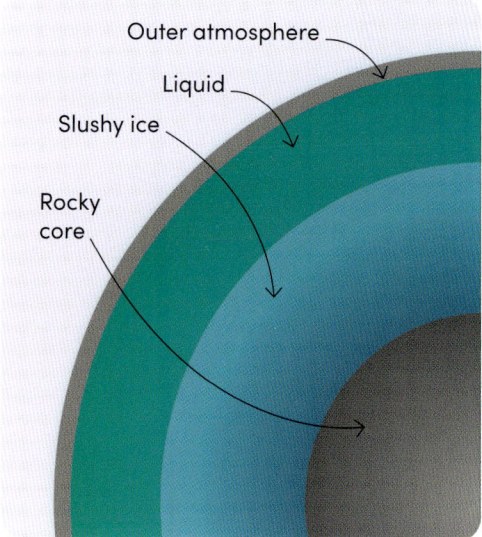

Outer atmosphere
Liquid
Slushy ice
Rocky core

Icy layers

Thick, cold gas in the planet's atmosphere turns liquid below its surface. Deeper inside, the liquid turns into slushy ice that moves around a solid core.

Uranus' rings are much narrower and darker than Saturn's.

Faint rings

Neptune has five main rings made up of dust and ice. Unlike Saturn, this ice giant's faint rings are almost impossible to see from Earth.

Picture taken by Voyager 2 shows three faint rings.

A LONG VOYAGE

Uranus and Neptune are so far away that only one spacecraft has visited them! Voyager 2 was launched in 1977, and zoomed past Uranus in 1986 and Neptune in 1989. It is now exploring the edge of the Solar System.

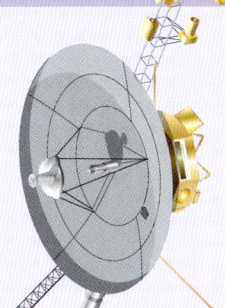

One of many measuring instruments on the spacecraft

Bright, white clouds drift around in the atmosphere.

Stormy world

The planet Neptune is the windiest place in the Solar System. High-speed winds blow through its atmosphere, sometimes creating giant storms that may last up to six Earth years.

A gas called methane gives Neptune its colour.

JUPITER
Ganymede
Callisto
Europa

Many moons

Earth is not the only planet that has a moon to keep it company. Moons are natural satellites: rocky or icy objects that stay close to planets, travelling in looping circles around them.

Lots of shapes

More than 270 moons orbit Saturn. Huge, round Titan is the biggest of them. The smaller moons aren't all round – some are even shaped like pasta or potatoes!

Pan

Hyperion

Smashed surface

Uranus has 28 moons, with five of them much bigger than the others. One moon, Miranda, has a surface that looks like it's been broken apart and then rearranged.

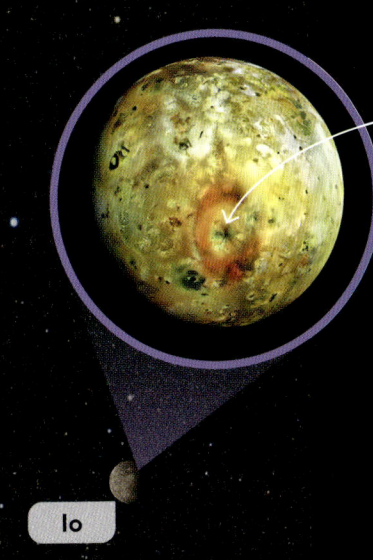

Io has at least 400 active volcanoes.

Io

Cluster of moons

Jupiter has at least 95 moons. Most of them are small, but four stand out: Io, Europa, Ganymede, and Callisto are much bigger than the rest. Ganymede is the biggest moon in the whole Solar System. Europa's underground ocean will be studied by the Europa Clipper spacecraft launched in 2024.

Titan

Beneath Titan's clouds

A thick layer of gases surrounds Titan. In 2005, a space probe called Huygens landed on its surface, and was able to take pictures of it.

Captured planet?

Neptune has at least 16 moons. The moon pictured here – Triton – is much bigger than the rest. Scientists think it may be a dwarf planet that was pulled into orbit by Neptune's gravity.

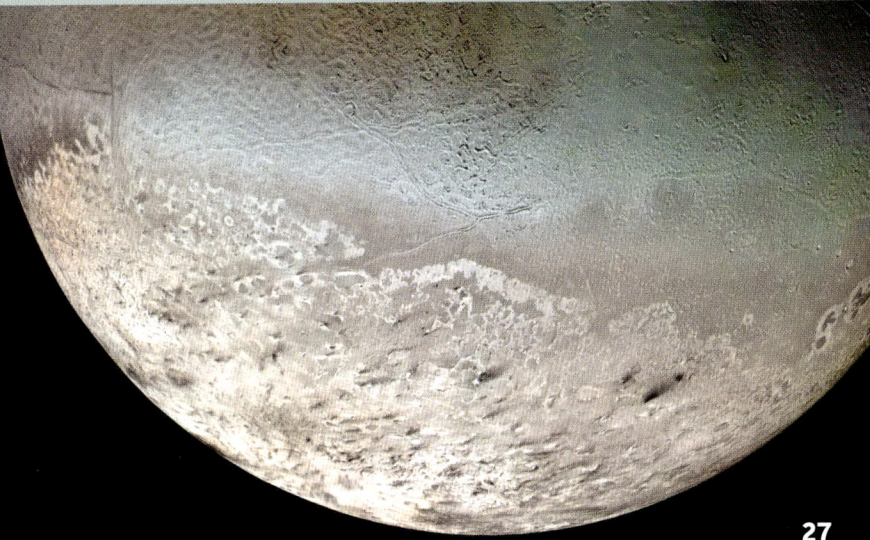

Frozen world
The largest known dwarf planet in our Solar System is Pluto. It has a hard, icy surface with liquid water underneath. Sometimes the water escapes to Pluto's surface as slushy ice.

Tombaugh Regio is a bright, heart-shaped region made of ice.

Speedy explorer
One of the fastest spacecraft ever launched, New Horizons flew past Pluto in 2015, a mere nine years after leaving Earth.

Mini planets
Ball-shaped objects smaller than planets that orbit the Sun are called dwarf planets. Most of them orbit the Sun in the Kuiper Belt – a doughnut-shaped region of space beyond Neptune.

Sedna takes 11,400 Earth years to make one trip around the Sun!

Eris

Haumea

Makemake

Sedna

Edge of the Solar System

If you flew from Earth on an aeroplane, it would take you more than 550 years to reach Neptune. Beyond it is a region of space called the Kuiper Belt – full of small, planet-like objects and icy comets. Even further out is the Oort Cloud, which is home to some of the oldest comets.

This photograph of Comet 67P was captured by the Rosetta spacecraft in 2014.

Icy wanderer

Comets are small objects made of rock, ice, and dust. When a comet comes close to the Sun in its orbit, it puffs out gas and dust. This creates a glowing cloud that sometimes stretches out into one or more long tails.

👁 DISTANT WORLD

Arrokoth is the most distant object visited by a spacecraft. New Horizons flew past it in 2019. This Kuiper Belt object is made of two rocky bodies fused together.

Giant bubble

A vast cloud of comets called the Oort Cloud surrounds our Solar System. The comets that come from this region may take millions of years to orbit the Sun.

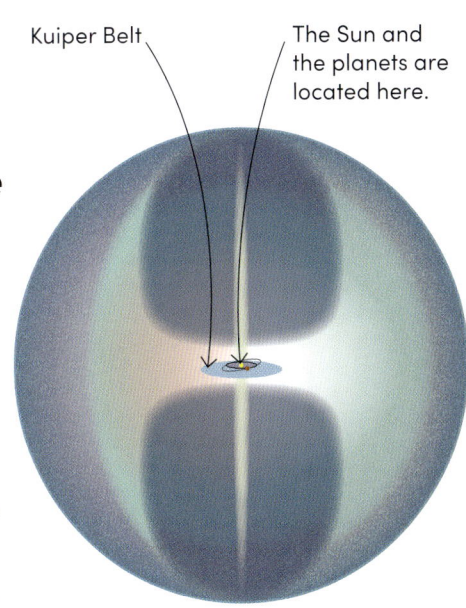

Kuiper Belt

The Sun and the planets are located here.

This computer-made picture of Kepler-62e is based on what scientists believe the exoplanet is like.

Studying exoplanets

Some exoplanets are quite similar to the planets in our own Solar System, while others are very different. Astronomers use clever tricks to measure the orbits of exoplanets, their sizes, and how much material they contain. This helps them imagine these distant alien worlds.

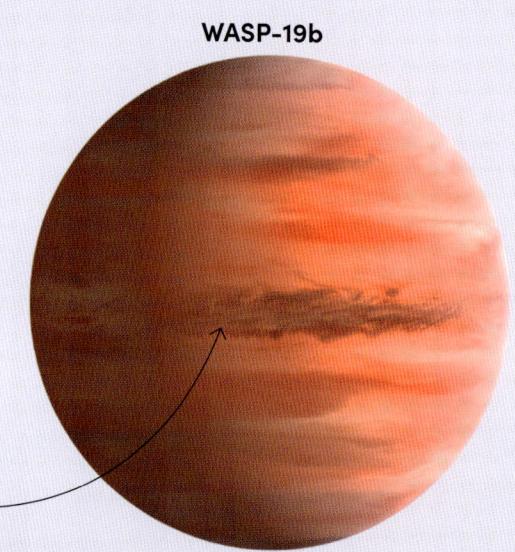

WASP-19b

WASP-19b is a hot gas giant that zips around its star in just 19 hours!

Exoplanets

Our Solar System has eight planets, but there are millions more in our galaxy alone. The planets outside our Solar System are called exoplanets, and many of them circle their own star.

Another Earth?

Is there alien life in space? Scientists don't know yet. But they study exoplanets to try and find signs of life. Kepler-62e is an exoplanet that is a little larger than Earth. It orbits its star at just the right distance – not too close or too far away. This means that it could have an atmosphere similar to Earth, liquid water, and suitable temperatures for life to flourish.

 FIRST PHOTO

It is hard to see exoplanets even with telescopes because they are usually drowned out by the light from their parent star. In 2004, astronomers finally captured the first image of an exoplanet (red object) orbiting a star called 2M1207 (blue object).

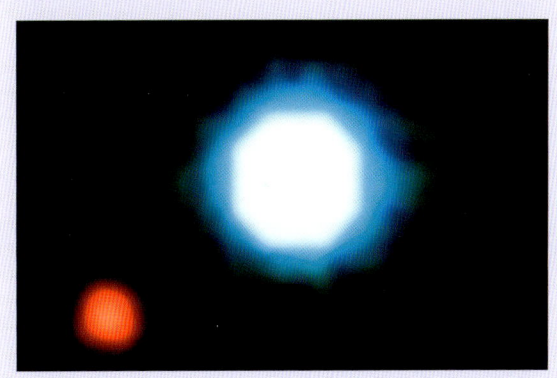

J1407B

The rings of the planet J1407b are 200 times wider than Saturn's rings.

55 Cancri e

The surface of the planet 55 Cancri e is covered in an ocean of molten lava.

Star birth
Dense clouds of gas and dust may slowly collapse under their own gravity to form new stars. These clouds are called nebulae. Many stars are being born in the Eagle Nebula (left).

Red giant
After billions of years, the star starts to run out of fuel. It brightens and swells up, becoming a red giant.

Shining star
Most stars have a hot, dense core and shine brightly for billions of years.

If a star is up to eight times as heavy as our Sun, it follows this path.

If a star is more than eight times as heavy as our Sun, it follows this path.

Life of stars

Just like people, stars change as they get older. How long a star shines for, the way that it dies, and what it leaves behind all depend on how much hydrogen fuel the star contains.

Supergiant
Heavyweight stars run out of fuel after just a few million years, and swell into unstable supergiants.

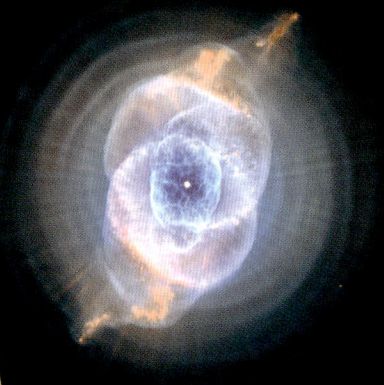

Planetary nebula
The red giant puffs off its outer layers into shells that glow for a few thousand years.

White dwarf
Once the star's outer layers are gone, the hot core is left as a "white dwarf".

Neutron star
A neutron star is the collapsed core of a monster star, blasting out beams of light and invisible radiation.

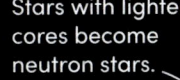

Stars with lighter cores become neutron stars.

Black hole
The heaviest cores collapse into black holes – objects whose gravity stops even light from escaping.

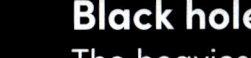

Stars with the heaviest cores become black holes.

Supernova
The star's core collapses suddenly, and shock waves tear the rest of the star apart in a huge explosion.

The biggest red supergiants can fit more than 5 billion Suns inside them.

Red supergiant

Types of stars

Next to the most gigantic stars, our Sun looks like a tiny dot! For most of a star's life its brightness depends on how much fuel it has – the biggest and brightest stars make the most energy. Towards the end of their lives, most stars grow brighter and then turn cooler and redder, as they run out of fuel.

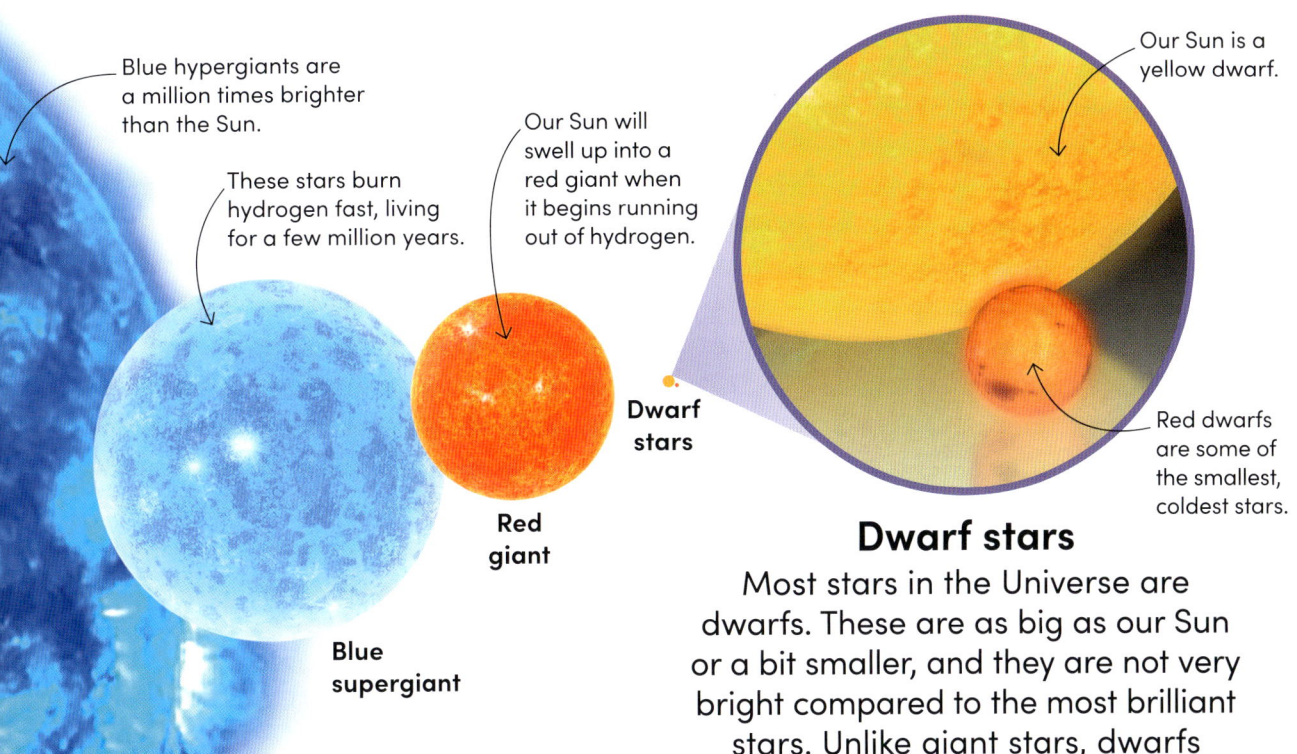

Blue hypergiants are a million times brighter than the Sun.

These stars burn hydrogen fast, living for a few million years.

Our Sun will swell up into a red giant when it begins running out of hydrogen.

Dwarf stars

Red giant

Blue supergiant

Blue hypergiant

Our Sun is a yellow dwarf.

Red dwarfs are some of the smallest, coldest stars.

Dwarf stars

Most stars in the Universe are dwarfs. These are as big as our Sun or a bit smaller, and they are not very bright compared to the most brilliant stars. Unlike giant stars, dwarfs don't die in a huge explosion.

Giant stars

The most massive stars in the Universe are old stars that have used up their hydrogen fuel and expanded like balloons. As their end draws near, giant stars may swallow nearby planets that are orbiting too close.

Fast facts

Supergiants are the rarest stars, while red dwarfs are the most common.

The closest star to Earth is the Sun.

The second-closest star to Earth is a red dwarf named Proxima Centauri. You cannot spot it without a telescope as its light is too faint.

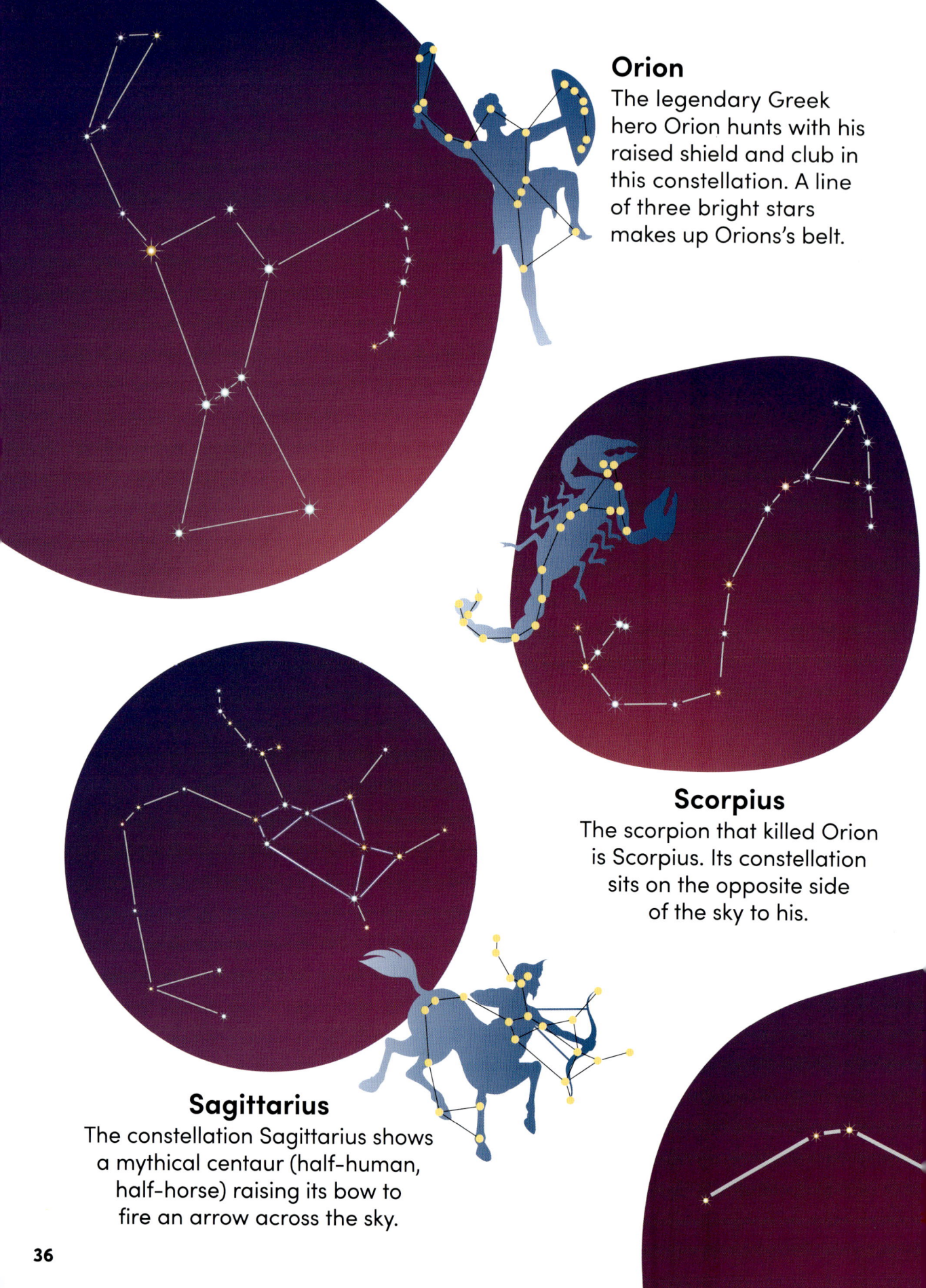

Orion
The legendary Greek hero Orion hunts with his raised shield and club in this constellation. A line of three bright stars makes up Orions's belt.

Scorpius
The scorpion that killed Orion is Scorpius. Its constellation sits on the opposite side of the sky to his.

Sagittarius
The constellation Sagittarius shows a mythical centaur (half-human, half-horse) raising its bow to fire an arrow across the sky.

Constellations

Stare at the stars in the night sky and you might just notice "shapes" formed by them. Astronomers can make out 88 different shapes in the sky, called constellations. Some can be seen clearly from the northern parts of Earth, while others are more clearly visible from the southern regions.

Cygnus
The swan Cygnus soars through the night sky with open wings. The star in its "tail" is one of the brightest in the Milky Way galaxy.

Ursa Major (Great Bear)
The majestic bear Ursa Major is one of the most commonly visible constellations in the night sky.

Hydra
Named after a many-headed monster serpent, Hydra looks like a giant snake slithering across the night sky. It is the largest of the 88 constellations.

Families of stars

A galaxy is an enormous family of stars, gas, and dust, all held together by the pull of gravity. An unthinkable number of galaxies make up our Universe.

Spiral galaxy (Andromeda)

Barred spiral galaxy (NGC 6956)

Elliptical galaxy (NGC 4150)

Irregular galaxy (Large Magellanic Cloud)

The Milky Way may contain as many as 400 billion stars.

Types of galaxies

Spiral galaxies look like whirlpools, with spiral arms sprouting from a bright core. Barred spirals are similar, but with a straight bar in the middle. Ellipticals are oval-shaped, while irregular galaxies have no shape at all.

Fast facts

Our galaxy is called the Milky Way.

Starlight from one side of our galaxy would take 100,000 years to reach the other side.

Our Solar System sits halfway along a small spiral arm called the Orion Spur.

Heavy heart
At the heart of our galaxy is a gigantic black hole, which weighs the same as 4 million Suns. Scientists were able to photograph it in 2024 using the Event Horizon Telescope.

Giant spiral
Our Milky Way is a large barred spiral galaxy. It has a star-packed central bar, with several arms that spiral out from the centre and rotate around it.

Part of the Milky Way in the night sky

Starry wonder
We live inside the Milky Way, so we cannot see its true shape. From Earth, it looks like a sparkling band of hazy light stretched out against the night sky.

All about the Universe

The Universe is everything! It contains all the planets, stars, and galaxies in space. It is huge, stretching out farther than we could ever see over distances so vast they are hard to imagine.

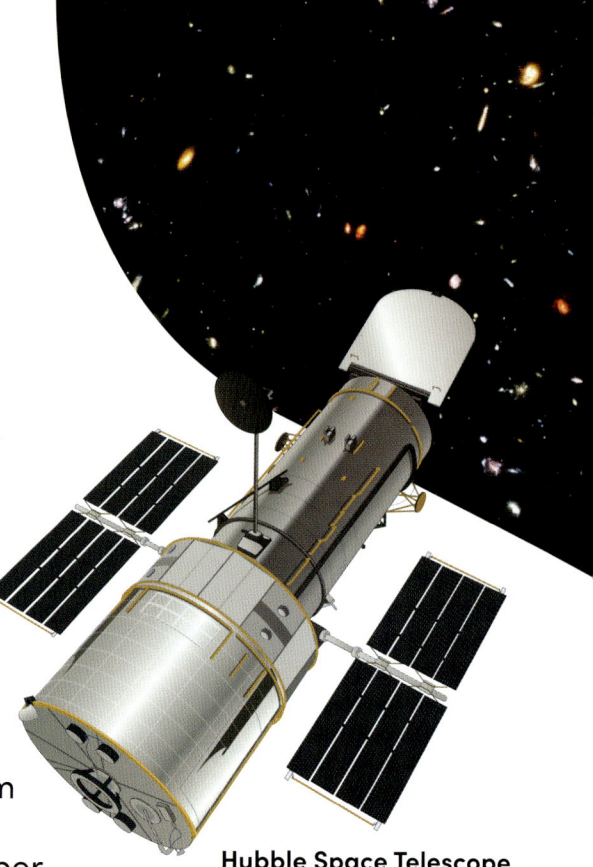

Eyes on the sky
Powerful telescopes can detect the faint light from faraway galaxies. This helps scientists look deeper into the Universe around us.

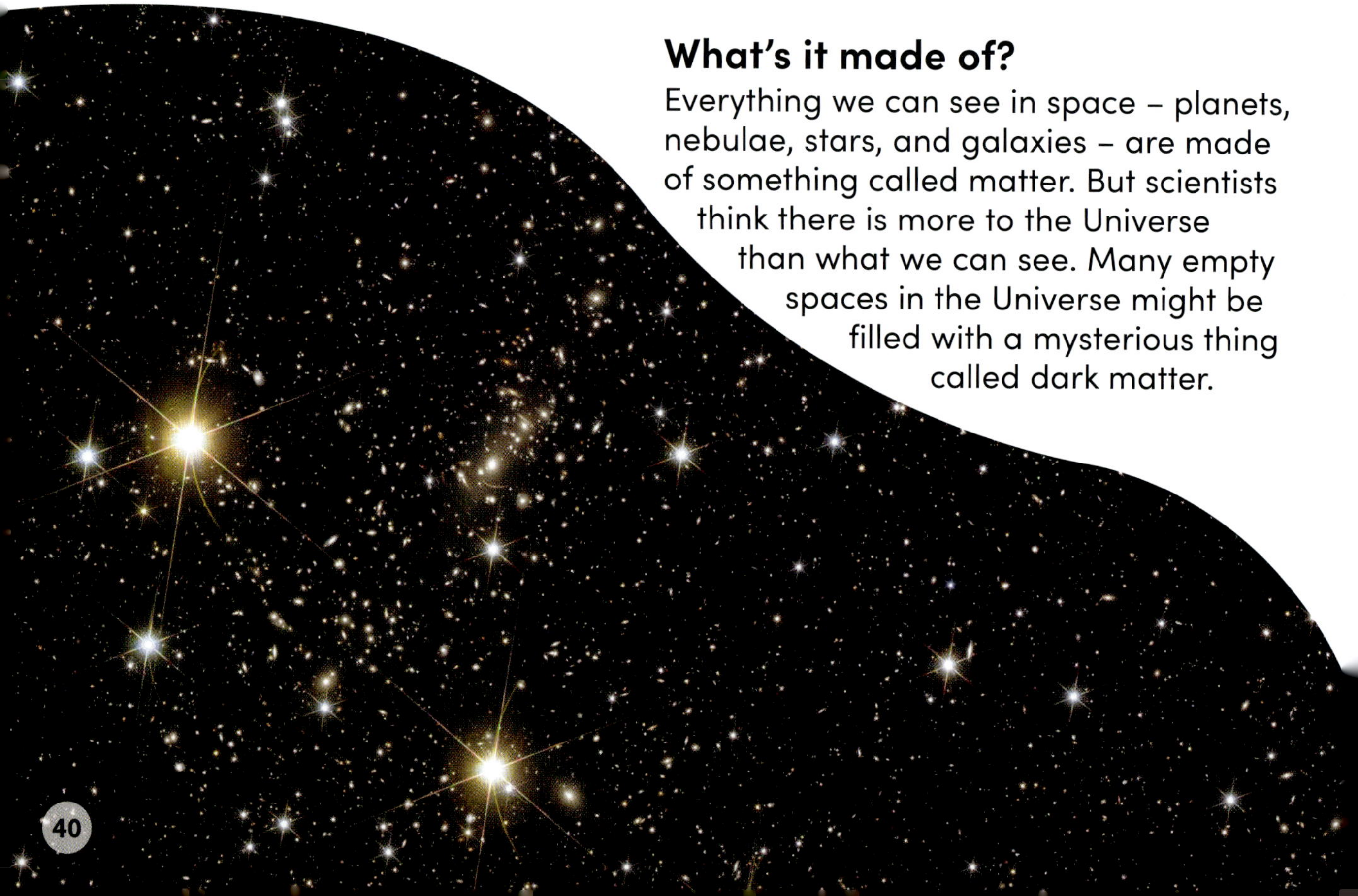

Hubble Space Telescope

What's it made of?
Everything we can see in space – planets, nebulae, stars, and galaxies – are made of something called matter. But scientists think there is more to the Universe than what we can see. Many empty spaces in the Universe might be filled with a mysterious thing called dark matter.

Far, far away
It can take millions or even billions of years for light from other galaxies to reach Earth. This means our pictures of the far-off Universe are snapshots of how it was in the distant past, not today.

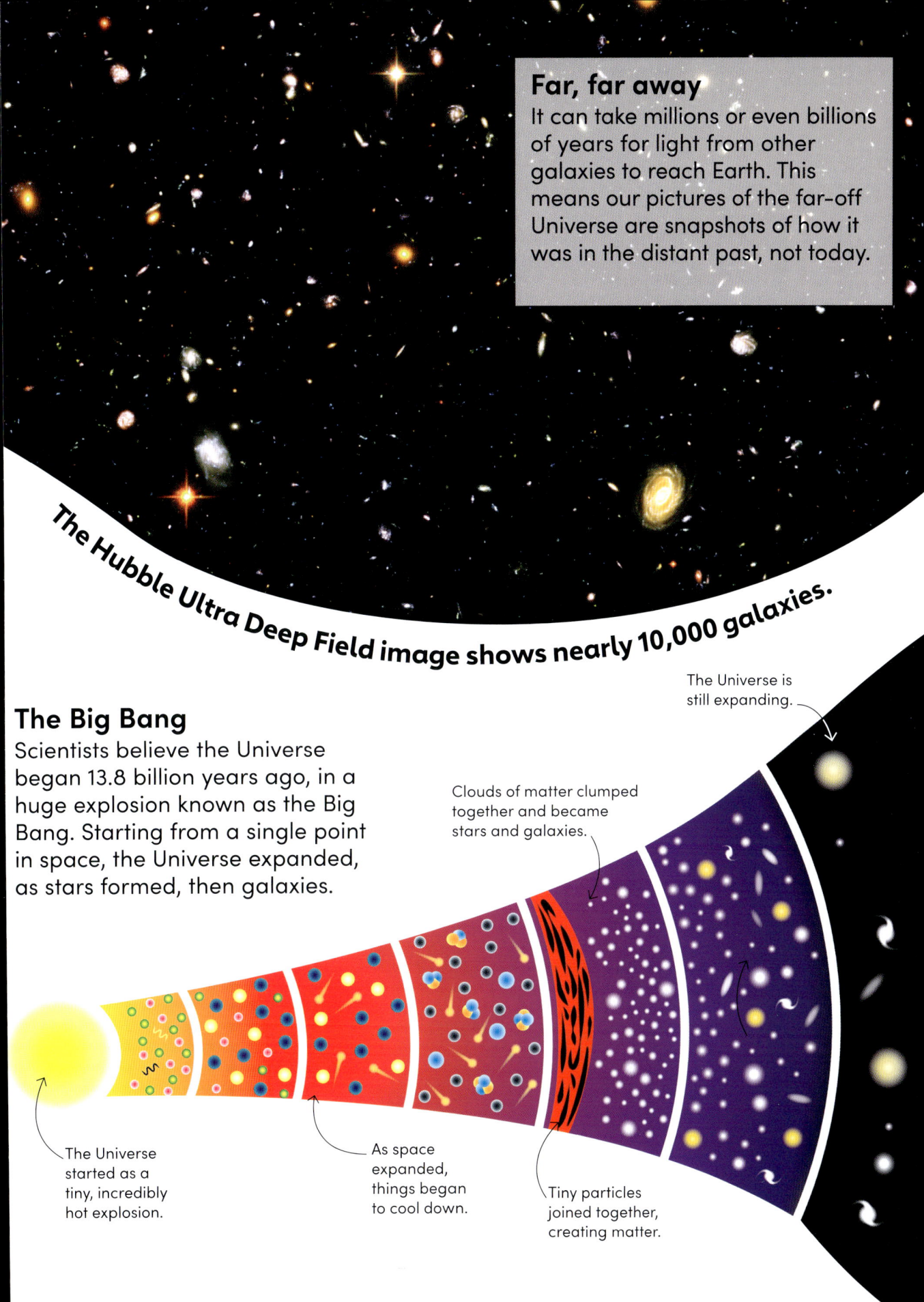

The Hubble Ultra Deep Field image shows nearly 10,000 galaxies.

The Big Bang
Scientists believe the Universe began 13.8 billion years ago, in a huge explosion known as the Big Bang. Starting from a single point in space, the Universe expanded, as stars formed, then galaxies.

The Universe is still expanding.

Clouds of matter clumped together and became stars and galaxies.

The Universe started as a tiny, incredibly hot explosion.

As space expanded, things began to cool down.

Tiny particles joined together, creating matter.

Exploring space

Getting into space is not easy! Spacecraft must travel at very high speeds to move away from Earth. To go further into space and towards other planets, they must move even faster.

Large rockets will power crewed spacecraft that take astronauts back to the Moon.

Rocket power

Spacecraft and cargo are sent to space on launch vehicles called rockets. To break free of Earth's gravity, a rocket needs huge amounts of power – this comes from burning fuel. The rocket falls away when its fuel is used up.

LAUNCH STAGES

Most rockets are made of "stages". Each stage has its own rocket engine and fuel tanks which fall away when the fuel is used up. Only the spacecraft or cargo makes the full journey into space. Some rockets, such as SpaceX's Falcon 9, are reusable – they carry extra fuel so they can return to Earth and be ready for another trip.

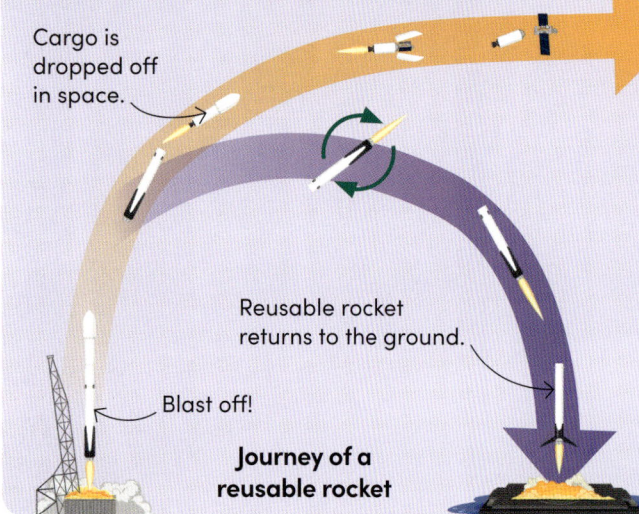

Cargo is dropped off in space.

Reusable rocket returns to the ground.

Blast off!

Journey of a reusable rocket

Delivery service

Most spacecraft only ever travel into orbit around Earth. They carry cargo, such as a space telescope, or transfer supplies and astronauts back and forth to a space station.

Taikonaut (Chinese astronaut) on a Shenzou craft heading to the Chinese Tiangong-1 space station.

Fast facts

The first human in space was Russian astronaut Yuri Gagarin.

In 1969, the Saturn V rocket sent the Apollo 11 mission to the Moon. US astronauts Neil Armstrong and Buzz Aldrin became the first humans to land on it. No human has been to the Moon since 1972.

US astronaut Peggy Whitson spent 675 days in total in space – the most among female astronauts.

Space rides

Some spacecraft take people into space just for fun. They carry space tourists up and out of Earth's atmosphere, then travel back to Earth without ever going around it.

Types of spacecraft

Some spacecraft leave Earth's orbit and head into space itself. There are several different types. Most of them are robotic and don't carry humans.

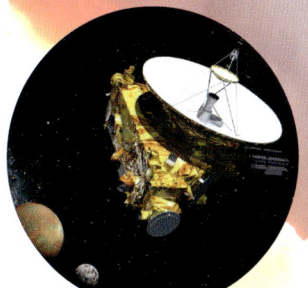

Flyby probes travel past their target without ever landing.

Orbiters enter orbit around their target, circling round it.

Landers touch down on the surface of a space object.

Rovers are wheeled vehicles that explore their target's surface.

A spacesuit protects an astronaut in space.

Spacewalk
When an astronaut in space leaves their spacecraft to do some research or repair work, it is called a spacewalk.

Life in orbit

At first, humans went into space for just a few hours or a few days, to see what it was like. Now, astronauts can spend weeks or months living and working in orbiting research spacecraft known as space stations.

 SPACE FOOD

Food to be eaten on a craft in space is packed in airtight containers to preserve it for a long time. Food packs might include different kinds of meat, rice, or nuts.

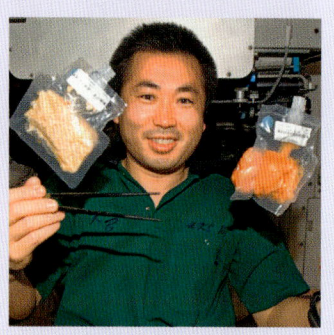

The station is made up of sections called modules, which contain labs and living spaces.

Space lab

The International Space Station (ISS) can fit around six astronauts, on missions of up to a year. Crews on space stations do experiments to try to learn more about Earth and space.

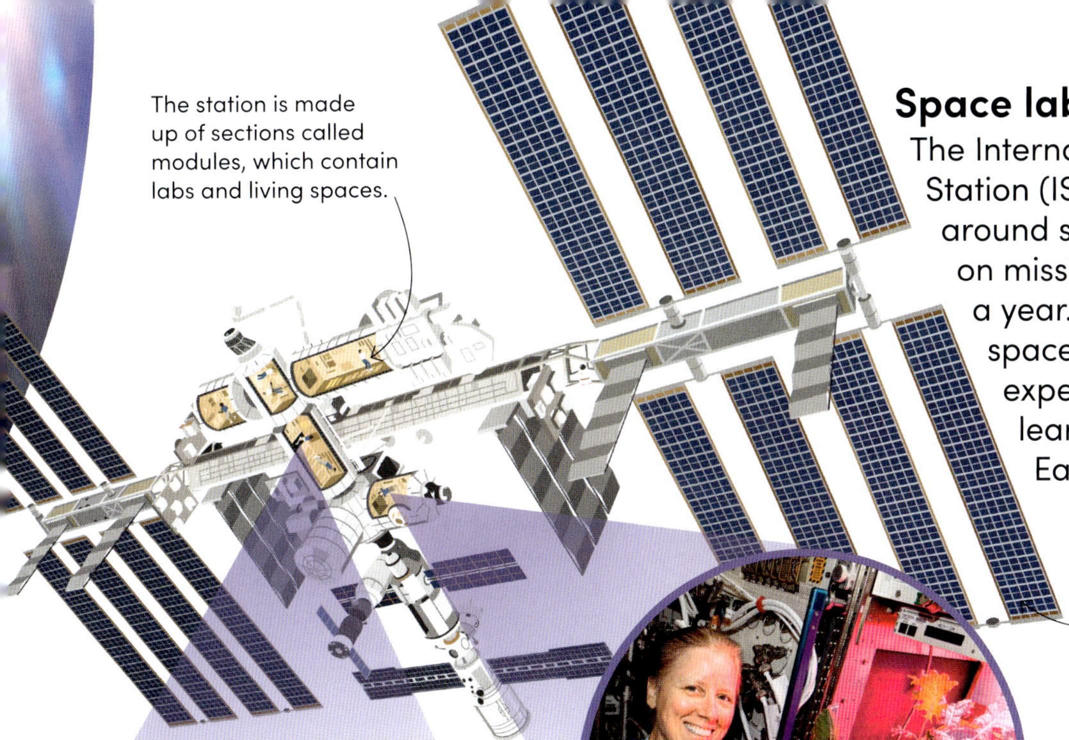

Huge solar panels make electricity.

This gardening experiment looks at how plants grow in space.

Astronauts run on a treadmill to keep fit.

Living in space

Astronauts on the ISS follow a regular daily routine. They have time to rest, sleep, and exercise. There are regular cleaning chores to do, too!

Taikonaut (Chinese astronaut) floats inside China's Tiangong space station.

Floating around

Inside a spacecraft orbiting Earth, gravity doesn't pull things downwards like it does on the ground. People and objects float around freely.

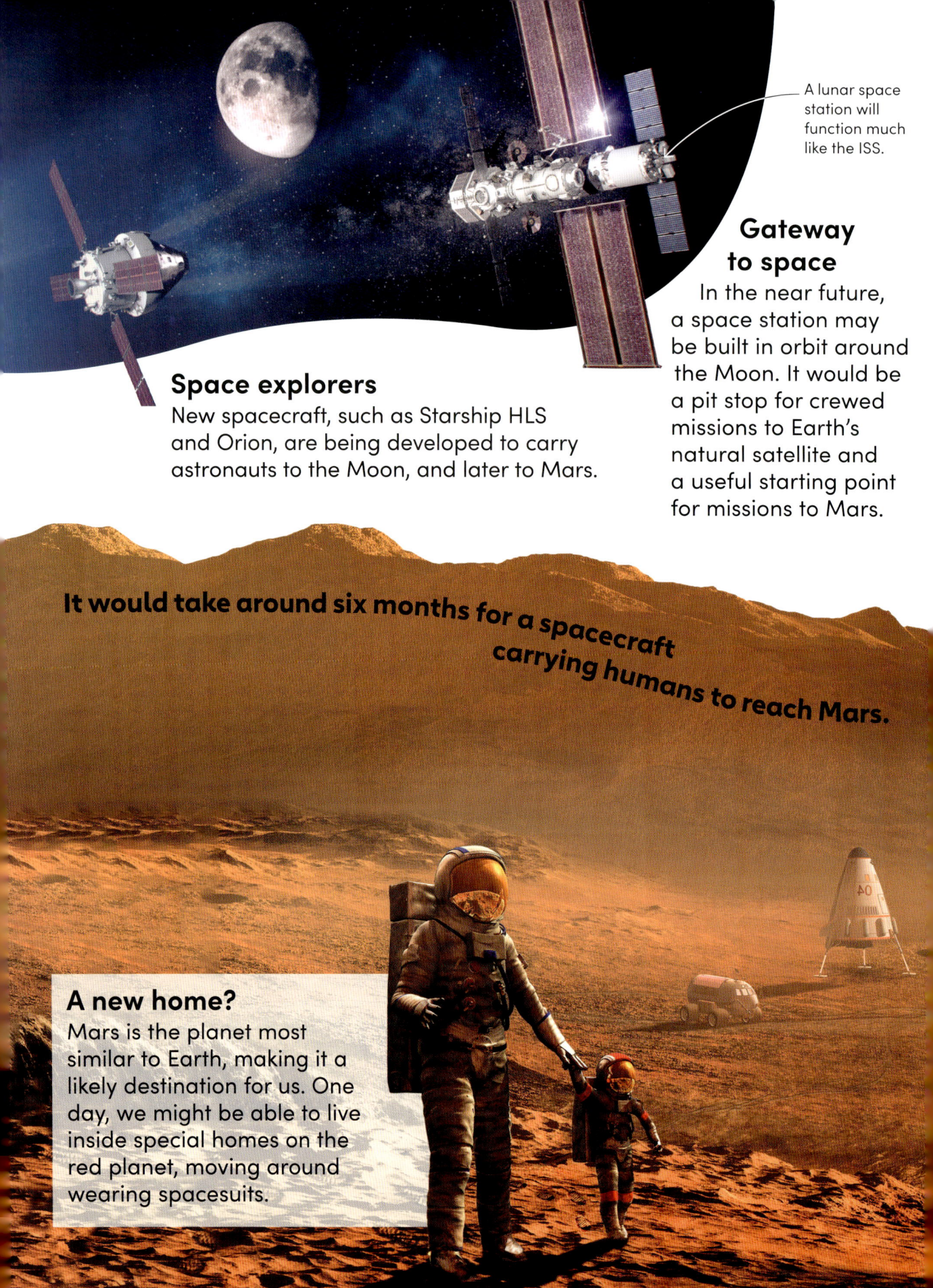

A lunar space station will function much like the ISS.

Gateway to space
In the near future, a space station may be built in orbit around the Moon. It would be a pit stop for crewed missions to Earth's natural satellite and a useful starting point for missions to Mars.

Space explorers
New spacecraft, such as Starship HLS and Orion, are being developed to carry astronauts to the Moon, and later to Mars.

It would take around six months for a spacecraft carrying humans to reach Mars.

A new home?
Mars is the planet most similar to Earth, making it a likely destination for us. One day, we might be able to live inside special homes on the red planet, moving around wearing spacesuits.

Our future in space

Humans have only travelled as far as the Moon. We are now trying to go back to the Moon and even further into space. Someday we might be able to live on the Moon or Mars, and explore the whole Solar System.

Spinning around
Future space stations might be able to spin around, creating an effect similar to Earth's gravity. This would allow astronauts to stay in space for longer.

Stargazers

A group of children want to see the stars through a big land telescope. But they need your help! Walk them through this maze of clues so they can reach their destination quickly.

The huge explosion that started the Universe was the
See page 41

The first rover to explore the far side of the Moon was
See page 9

A huge storm on Jupiter 1.3 times bigger than Earth is the
See page 20

Start

What's this?

Test your space knowledge by identifying these close-up pictures. The clues will help.

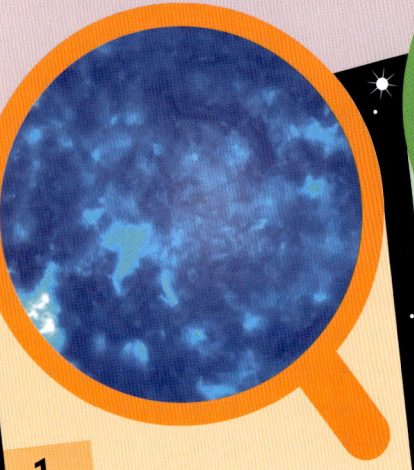

1
- This is a type of giant star.
- It is a million times brighter than our Sun.

2
- The tallest mountain in the Solar System can be seen on this planet.
- Its surface is covered in red dust.

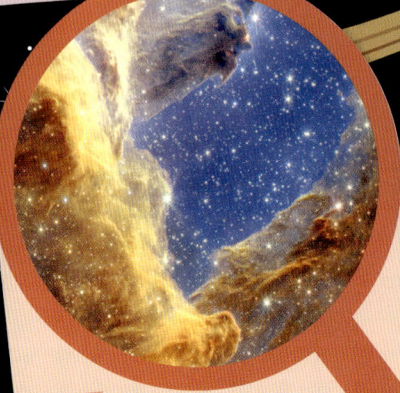

3
- New stars are born in this nebula.
- It is packed with gas and dust.

4
- The rings of this planet are made of ice.
- It was studied by the Cassini spacecraft.

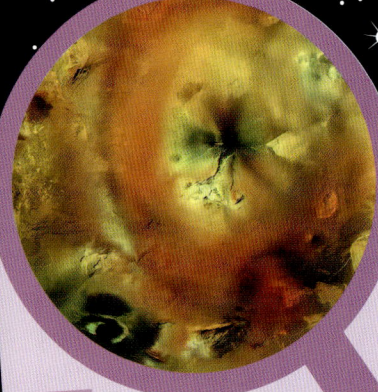

5
- This is one of Jupiter's larger moons.
- Its surface is covered in volcanoes.

6
- We live in this galaxy.
- It has a star-packed central bar.

7
- China is home to this large telescope.
- Its dish is as big as 30 football fields.

8
- Not even light can escape the strong gravity of this thing.
- It sits at the heart of our galaxy.

9
- This is the largest planet in the Solar System.
- It protects Earth by pulling in many passing comets.

10
- This is the largest constellation in the night sky.
- It looks like a giant snake.

Answers: 1.Blue hypergiant 2.Mars 3.Eagle Nebula 4.Saturn 5.Io 6.Milky Way 7.FAST radio telescope 8.Black hole 9.Jupiter 10.Hydra

51

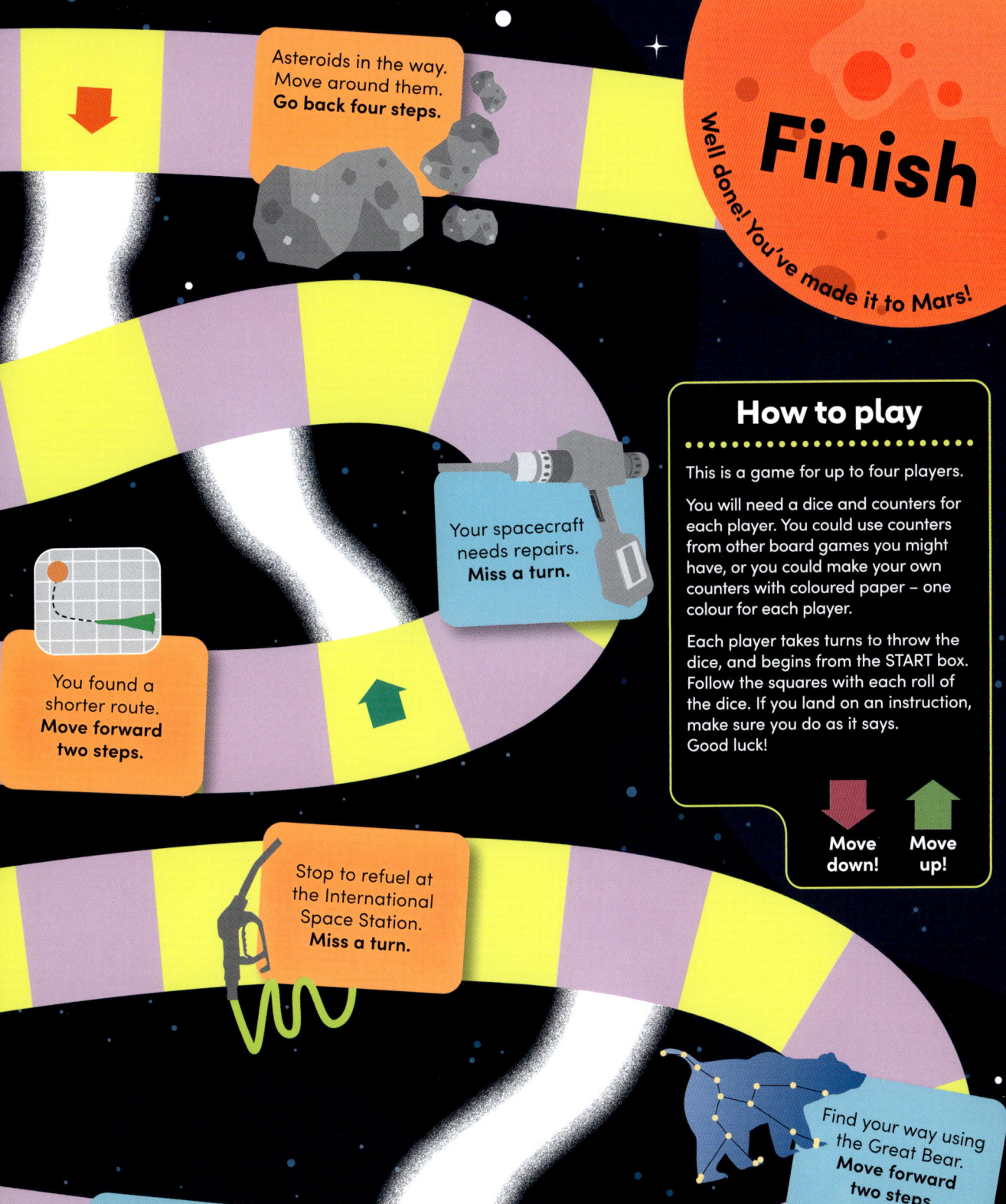

Glossary

Air A mixture of gases that forms planet Earth's atmosphere.

Alien life Living things that might be found in other places beyond Earth.

Asteroid A space rock.

Astronaut A person who travels to space.

Astronomer A space scientist. An astronomer studies space and objects in it.

Atmosphere A layer of gases held in place around an object in space by its gravity.

Big Bang An event that triggered the formation of the Universe around 13.8 billion years ago.

Black hole An incredibly dense object with gravity so strong that nothing – not even light – can escape it.

Comet An object made of rocky dust, snow, and ice. Comets travel on very long orbits around the Sun.

Constellation A shape formed by stars visible in the night sky.

Core The stuff that makes up the centre of a star, planet, dwarf planet, or moon.

Corona The atmosphere of a star, such as the Sun, made of very hot gases.

Crater A large, bowl-shaped dent in the surface of a moon or planet.

Crust The hard, rocky layer at the surface of a rocky body such as a moon, dwarf planet, or planet.

Dwarf planet A sphere-shaped body that orbits the Sun, but which is too small to be classed as a planet.

Exoplanet A planet outside the Solar System that may orbit a star.

Gravity The natural, invisible force of attraction between objects – such as the pull between the Sun and Earth. Things stay in orbit around other things because of gravity.

Ice giant A large planet with outer layers of gas and liquid, and an interior mostly made of slushy ice.

Launch vehicle A large rocket used to launch spacecraft and cargo into space. Launch vehicles are powered by engines, which burn fuel to push them forwards.

Lunar To do with the Moon.

Martian To do with Mars.

Meteor The streak of light made by a space rock as it burns up when travelling through Earth's atmosphere.

Meteorite A space rock that hits the surface of a moon, dwarf planet, or planet.

Moon A natural object in space that orbits a dwarf planet or planet.

Nebula A cloud of gas and dust in space. Stars form in some nebulae. Some dying stars may create a nebula.

Observatory A large building for housing a telescope.

Orbit The name for the journey that one object takes around another due to the gravity between them. Also the path taken by an object when looping around another.

Oxygen A gas that plants and nearly all animals on Earth need to survive.

Particles Tiny fragments of material that make up everything in the Universe and are sometimes blown out from objects like stars.

Planet A large, ball-shaped object in space that orbits a star. The planets of our Solar System orbit a star called the Sun.

Satellite Any object in space that orbits another object. Natural satellites of planets or dwarf planets are called moons.

Shooting star Another name for a meteor.

Solar To do with the Sun.

Solar System The set of planets (and their moons), dwarf planets, asteroids, and comets moving in orbits around the Sun.

Spacecraft A vehicle for travelling in space. Spacecraft may be crewed or uncrewed (robotic or remotely controlled from Earth).

Space probe A robot spacecraft programmed to explore distant places in our Solar System.

Space station A large spacecraft that stays in orbit around an object in space. It is used as a temporary home by astronauts who live and work in space.

Star A very large, spinning ball of scorching hot, burning gas. Stars produce light and heat energy. The Sun is our closest star.

Telescope An instrument that makes distant objects, such as those in space, appear brighter and larger.

Index

ABC
Apollo 8
Arrokoth 29
Asteroid Belt 12, 18, 19
asteroids 13, 18–19
astronauts 8, 42, 43, 44–45, 46
atmosphere 4, 17, 24
auroras 11, 21
Big Bang 41
black holes 33, 39
Cassini 22, 23
Ceres 19
comets 13, 21, 29
constellations 6, 36–37
craters 9, 14

DE
dark matter 40
dwarf planets 19, 27, 28
dwarf stars 33, 35
Earth 4, 8, 10, 11, 14
eclipse, solar 10
Europa 27
Europa Clipper 27
exoplanets 30–31
exploration 9, 16, 19, 25, 28, 42–43

GHI
galaxies 31, 38–39, 41
Ganymede 27
gas giants 21, 22, 30
giant stars 32, 33, 35
gravity 4, 16, 21, 27, 33, 38
Hayabusa2 19
Huygens 27
hydrogen 5, 11, 35
ice 22, 24, 25, 28, 29
Ingenuity 16
International Space Station (ISS) 44–45
Io 27

JKL
Juno 21
Jupiter 20–21, 27
Kepler-62e 31
Kuiper Belt 28, 29
life 4, 10, 31, 47
light years 5

MNO
Mars 16–17, 46
matter 40, 41
Mercury 14
meteorites 18
meteors 19
Milky Way 38, 39
Miranda 26
Moon, Earth's 4, 8–9, 43, 46
moons 8–9, 16, 23, 26–27
nebulae 32, 33
Neptune 24, 25, 27
neutron stars 33
New Horizons 28, 29
Oort Cloud 29
Orion spacecraft 46

PRS
Parker Solar Probe 10
Perseverance 16
Phobos 16
planets 12, 13, 31
Pluto 28
probes 9, 10, 16, 43
radiation 6, 7
rings 22–23, 25, 31
rockets 42, 43
Rosetta 29
rovers 9, 16, 43
Saturn 22–23, 26
seasons, Earth's 10
shooting stars 19
Solar System 12–13, 38
spacecraft 8, 9, 10, 14, 16, 19, 21, 23, 25, 27, 28, 29, 42–46
space stations 43, 44–45, 46, 47
stars 5, 6, 10, 32–37
Starship HLS 46
Sun 4, 10–11, 35
supergiants 32, 34, 35
supernova 33

TUVW
telescopes 5, 6–7, 24, 40, 43
Titan 26, 27
Triton 27
Universe 40–41
Uranus 14, 24, 25, 26
Venus 14, 15
volcanoes 15, 17, 27
Voyager 2 25
water 4, 28
wind 15, 25

Acknowledgments

DK would like to thank the following people for their help with making the book: Lizzie Munsey for text contributions; Aashirwad Jain, Shahid Qureshi, and Bipasha Roy for editorial assistance; Revati Anand for design assistance; Priya Singh and Samrajkumar S for picture research administration; and Carron Brown for proofreading and indexing.

The publisher would like to thank the following for their kind permission to reproduce their photographs:

(Key: a-above; b-below/bottom; c-centre; f-far; l-left; r-right; t-top)

Adobe Stock: Artvi 30br, Blue Jean Images 6cl; **Alamy Stock Photo:** Associated Press / JAXA 19tr, Associated Press / NASA / JPL-Caltech / ASU / MSSS 16cla, Joshimer Biñas 27tl, 50crb, Drew Buckley 5b, Connect Images / Victoria Zeffert 31cr, DPA Picture Alliance Archive 10c, Michele Falzone 7br, Mark Garlick 13cr, Geopix 43cr, 44br, Imaginechina Limited 43tl, Imago / Ou Dongqu 6-7t, 51tr, NASA / ESA / STScI / Luc Novovitch 2-3tc, 20-21bc, 43bc, NASA Image Collection 9tl, 28cra, 43bl, NASA Photo 45ca, 46tl, RGB Ventures / SuperStock / Tony Hallas 18tl, Science Photo Library / Mark Garlick 10bl, 12-13tl, 47tr, Stocktrek Images, Inc. 9cl, 31tr, Stocktrek Images, Inc. / Alan Dyer 39crb, Stocktrek Images, Inc. / Fahad Sulehria 8tc, Stocktrek Images, Inc. / Roth Ritter 38cla, Stocktrek Images, Inc. / Steven Hobbs 46-47b, Stocktrek Images, Inc. / Walter Myers 17tr, 50ca, SuperStock / RGB Ventures / NASA 26cr, Ognyan Trifonov 45crb, Westend61 GmbH 4bc, Westend61 GmbH / Martin Rietze 38cb; **Depositphotos Inc:** Blueringmedia 42bl, Robertsrob 4tl; **Dorling Kindersley:** NASA / Peter Bull 22br; **Dreamstime.com:** Ciniangela 24clb, Edwinmostert 18tr, Sebastian Kaulitzki 24r, LoveEmployee 31bl, Macrovector 32 (x3), Natkapad 5tl, Michael Pelin 4br, Alexander Shalamov 11bl, Tatsiana Volskaya 52-53 (Background); **ESA:** ESA / Euclid / Euclid Consortium / NASA, image processing by J.-C. Cuillandre (CEA Paris-Saclay), G. Anselmi 40b, JAXA BepiColombo 14clb; **ESA / Hubble:** ESA / Hubble & NASA, C. Murray 54-55t, Hubble Space Telescope Comet Team and NASA / ESA 21tr, NASA, ESA, C.R. O'Dell (Vanderbilt University), and M. Meixner, P. McCullough, and G. Bacon (Space Telescope Science Institute) 6bc, NASA, ESA, P. McGill (Univ. of California, Santa Cruz and University of Cambridge), K. Sahu (STScI), J. Depasquale (STScI) 33tr, NASA, HEIC and The Hubble Heritage Team (STScI / AURA) 33tl; **ESO:** EHT Collaboration 39tr, 51cl, ESO / VISTA / J. Emerson / Cambridge Astronomical Survey Unit 1, 6br; **Getty Images:** Eerik 15bl, Future Publishing / CFOTO 9b, Science Photo Library / Nemes Laszlo 26-27t; **Getty Images / iStock:** 3DSculptor 42-43, Nadzeya Dzivakova 14br, Robertsrob 20tr; **Japan Aerospace Exploration Agency (JAXA):** PLANET-C Project Team 15cr; **NASA:** 7cl, 8cr, 17cla, 18-19 (Background), 44-45t, 52crb, DOE / Fermi LAT Collaboration, CXC / SAO / JPL-Caltech / Steward / O. Krause et al., and NRAO / AUI 33clb, Enhanced image by Kevin M. Gill (CC-BY) based on images provided courtesy of NASA / JPL-Caltech / SwRI / MSSS. 20, 51cl, ESA / NASA / JPL / University of Arizona 27c, ESA / Rosetta / MPS for OSIRIS Team MPS / UPD / LAM / IAA / SSO / INTA / UPM / DASP / IDA 29cra, ESA, and D. Jones (University of California – Santa Cruz); Processing: Gladys Kober (NASA / Catholic University of America) 38ca, ESA, CSA, STScI; Joseph DePasquale (STScI), Anton M. Koekemoer (STScI), Alyssa Pagan (STScI). 32tl, 50cra, JHUAPL / SwRI 28tl, Johns Hopkins University Applied Physics Laboratory / Arizona State University / Carnegie Institution of Washington 14tl, Johns Hopkins University Applied Physics Laboratory / Carnegie Institution of Washington 14tr, Johns Hopkins University Applied Physics Laboratory / Southwest Research Institute / Roman Tkachenko 29bl, JPL 15cla, 22-23t, 25cla, 50cb, JPL / University of Arizona / University of Idaho 27cl, JPL-Caltech 3br, 19cla, 23cr, 33c, 33br, 38-39c, 51cl, JPL-Caltech / MSSS 16b, JPL-Caltech / MSSS / Texas A&M Univ. 17bl, JPL-Caltech / Space Science Institute 23bl, 26c, Kevin Reardon (National Solar Observatory), Lucia Kleint (BAER Institute) 10tr, NASA / JPL-Caltech / CNES / IPGP / Imperial College / Cornell 43bc (Landers), NASA and the Hubble Heritage Team (STScI / AURA) / NASA / ESA, John Clarke (University of Michigan) 21crb, NASA Johnson 8bl, NASA, ESA, R.M. Crockett (University of Oxford, U.K.), S. Kaviraj (Imperial College London and University of Oxford, U.K.), J. Silk (University of Oxford), M. Mutchler (Space Telescope Science Institute, Baltimore, USA), R. O'Connell (University of Virginia, Charlottesville, USA), and the WFC3 Scientific Oversight Committee 38clb, NASA, ESA, S. Beckwith (STScI) and the HUDF Team 40-41t, NASA's Goddard Space Flight Center 34-35c, 50cla, SDO 10-11t; **Science Photo Library:** John Chumack 29cr, David Ducros 5cra, Mark Garlick 35ca, NASA 45cl, NASA / JPL / USGS 27br, US Geological Survey 26bl, Victor Habbick Visions 28br; **Shutterstock.com:** Beyond Space 12cr, Brannik 34l, BreizhAtao 28b, Raymond Cassel 43br

Cover images: *Front:* **123RF.com:** Leonello Calvetti cb/ (Earth), Solarseven tl; **Adobe Stock:** Dottedyeti clb/ (Asteroids), Elen31 tr/ (Moon); **Dorling Kindersley:** Andy Crawford ca, NASA tr; **Dreamstime.com:** Konstantin Shaklein tc/ (Space Launch), Martijn De Vries cra; **ESA:** ATG Medialab c/ (Webb Spacecraft), ESA / Hubble & NASA, CC BY 4.0 bc/ (Stars), NASA / ESA, Hans Van Winckel (Catholic University of Leuven, Belgium) and Martin Cohen (University of California) c/ (Nebula), NASA, ESA, A. Simon (Goddard Space Flight Center), and M. H. Wong (University of California, Berkeley) and the OPAL team; CC BY 4.0 bc; **ESO:** NASA crb/ (Deimos); **Getty Images / iStock:** Adventtr cr; **NASA:** br, ESA / Herschel / PACS / SPIRE / J. Fritz, U. Gent; X-ray: ESA / XMM Newton / EPIC / W. Pietsch, MPE cb, JPL crb, JPL-Caltech cla/ (Milky Way), NASA / JPL-Caltech bl, NASA Goddard tc, c, NASA, NOAO, ESA, and the Hubble Helix Nebula Team, M. Meixner (STScI), and T.A. Rector (NRAO) clb; *Back:* **Adobe Stock:** Dottedyeti cla; **Dorling Kindersley:** London Planetarium / James Stevenson bl, Science Museum, London / Geoff Dann tr, Science Museum, London / James Stevenson cr; **Dreamstime.com:** Banjong Khanyai bc/ (Satellite Dish); **ESA / Hubble:** NASA / ESA and The Hubble Heritage Team (AURA / STScI). clb; **NASA:** bc, ESA, Joel Kastner (RIT) br, JPL / University of Arizona cra, JPL / USGS crb, NASA, ESA, and K. Noll (STScI) / The Hubble Heritage Team (STScI / AURA) tc